NORTH
B

by James Hogan

‖SAMUEL FRENCH‖

ISBN 978-0-573-00060-7

concordtheatricals.co.uk
concordtheatricals.com

FOR AMATEUR PRODUCTION ENQUIRIES

UNITED KINGDOM AND WORLD
EXCLUDING NORTH AMERICA
licensing@concordtheatricals.co.uk

020-7054-7298

Each title is subject to availability from Concord Theatricals,
depending upon country of performance.

This work is published by Samuel French, an imprint of Concord Theatricals Ltd.

The Professional Rights in this play are controlled by United Agents LLP, 12-26 Lexington Street, London W1F 0LE.

USE OF COPYRIGHTED MUSIC

USE OF COPYRIGHTED THIRD-PARTY MATERIALS

IMPORTANT BILLING AND CREDIT REQUIREMENTS

KING'S HEAD THEATRE

King's Head Theatre is a purpose-built, wheelchair accessible theatre with a 200-seat flexible auditorium and 50-seat cabaret space off Upper St, Islington which showcases a wide range of performance styles from plays to musicals, to opera & cabaret, to drag & comedy.

Established in 1970, King's Head Theatre was the oldest pub theatre in the UK until it closed its doors in August 2023. For 53 years the theatre was housed in the back room of the King's Head Pub on Upper Street, before opening the new space in Islington Square right behind the pub theatre in January 2024.

Under Artistic Director & Founder Dan Crawford, whose tenure lasted 35 years until his death in 2005, the theatre became known as a breeding ground for new talent and great work. Renowned actors like Maureen Lipman, Hugh Grant, Jennifer Saunders, Dawn French, Alan Rickman & Richard E Grant all performed at the theatre, and a number of productions transferred to the West End and Broadway, premiering work from writers such as Steven Berkoff, Tom Stoppard, Bryony Lavery and Victoria Wood.

In 2010, the Olivier Award-winning company Opera UpClose Productions became the theatre's resident company for four years, and with Adam Spreadbury-Maher as Artistic Director, turned the King's Head into "London's Little Opera House", winning an Olivier Award for La Boheme in the Best New Opera category.

The theatre is a home for a new wave of theatre makers, with a focus on work which is joyful, irreverent, colourful & queer.

SUPPORT KING'S HEAD THEATRE – Angels of Angel Production Fund

The Angels of Angel Production fund is a fund that is specifically used to create and produce new work in our new theatre. Your donation won't just support the creation of one production, but an ongoing range of productions. All ticket income earned from the show will be put back into the fund and used to capitalise the next one.

Support us by joining our Network of Angels or Sponsor a Stair from our 53 year history.

Find out more www.kingsheadtheatre.com

NORTHBOUND BOY was first produced by Peter Darney and Northbound Productions at the King's Head Theatre on 13th August 2024. The cast and creative team was as follows:

KEN . . . . Neil Ashton
RORY . . . . Cormac Hyde-Corrin
IVY . . . . Sarah Moyle

CREATIVE TEAM

Writer | James Hogan
Director | Alex Jackson
Producers | Peter Darney; Northbound Productions
Set and costume designer | Cory Shipp
Lighting Designer | Sherry Coenen
Stage Manager | Gwenan Bain
Production Manager | Tom Naylor
Casting Directors | Emma Sylvester and Jessica Jefferies
Cover Design | Steph Payne
Sound Designer | Sonum Batra
Associate Sound Designer | Alan Short

CHARACTERS

KEN – (43) off-duty policeman
RORY – (19) M6 hitchhiker
IVY – (65) Ken's aunt

SETTING

Motorway services area
Ken's house on the Lancashire Moors

Scene One
Motorway services on the M6

(**RORY**, *nineteen, sitting at a table. Ken's empty cup close by.*)

(*Rory's rucksack and cardboard placard are on the floor. He wears military-style camos and a khaki beanie. He looks like a squaddie.*)

(**KEN**, *forty-three, approaches carrying a latte. He puts it on the table.*)

KEN. Those kids up there; large this, large that, giant Pepsi. Wallops your credit card.

RORY. If you've got one.

KEN. Fast food theme park, food, drink and gambling – slot machines. How to grab your money!

RORY. Clean and dry, mate.

(**KEN** *sits.*)

KEN. Latte, right?

RORY. Mega.

KEN. Mega?

RORY. Yeah, defo. Long queue, innit?

KEN. All on camera. CCTV, easy to spot villains, see? Face recognition.

RORY. Who?

KEN. Villains. They need comfort stops like the rest of us.

RORY. Nah, *outdoor* pissers.

KEN. Really? Think about that. Take as long as you like.

RORY. Ah, you mean if they...

KEN. Exactly. Villains, robbers, fraudsters, ever among us. You're on a bus, who's sat next to you? A serial killer? Anybody!

RORY. Covid? Down my end we all know each other. If not, who are they? Wide boys. All of 'em carry tools. Machetes.

KEN. And make no mistake. All of 'em known to the police.

RORY. Where I'm stayin', all he does is lie in bed and watch Superman. D'you like sci-fi? Aliens are also among us. I believe that. Aliens from Mars and far galaxies. The Universe ain't empty. Stands to reason.

KEN. There's no life on Mars. The studios rewrote the scripts ages ago. Drink up.

(**RORY** *sips the latte.*)

I reckon you could live in 'ere. Eat, drink, shop, cashpoint, toilets, change the baby, sleep in a motel.

RORY. Live on a motorway? Y'jokin'. Nightmare.

KEN. It's all laid on, no dishes, no cleaning up. Life without responsibility.

RORY. Scenery ain't much. Where do *you* live then?

KEN. Open country. No Covid, no noise, no floods, no pollution, no villains. Well, as long as you get an alarm system. I've just put one in.

RORY. Rant not over.

KEN. OK. I'll shut up. Roy, did you say?

RORY. Rory.

KEN RORY. My car's charging up, about ten minutes, OK?

RORY. Electric car chargers. Robots from outer space. Positronic brains. Indestructable unless you nuke them.

KEN. *(Beat.)* Really? You watch too many sci-fi movies.

RORY. TV. Can't afford cinemas or the bus. I asked my dad for the train fare. Stingy sod wouldn't breathe out unless he has to.

KEN. Spent all your money on slots?

RORY. Wanna buy me bucket o' chicken? *(Beat.)* Just sayin'.

KEN. *(Beat.)* Where y'from?

RORY. South London. Took ages. No one stops in this weather. Y'can't ask in'ere. Security. I done a lap round. Security jump out of nowhere.

KEN. Act like we know each other. *(Beat.)* Go on, talk to me.

RORY. Oh, 'ello, 'ello, nice to meet you, Mister.

KEN. The staff here know me. I'm off duty. Keep talking.

RORY. D'you work 'ere then?

KEN. Passing through incognito.

RORY. Where's your shades? Film star? Footballer? No you're too old.

KEN. *(Takes the hit.)* Fly-weight boxing.

RORY. Boxing champion?

KEN. Come on, talk like we're family. Ditch the Blackpool card. *I'll* take you there if you behave yourself. I mean that. Behave.

RORY. What have I done wrong?

KEN. I think you know!

RORY. No, what?

KEN. You took a risk back there. Don't you realise?

RORY. So did you.

KEN. You want a lift? I say cool it.

RORY. I see. Conditions apply.

> (**RORY** *bins the placard.*)

> (**KEN** *pulls his cap down to cover his face.*)

(Returning.) Thanks for the latte.

KEN. Drink up. Latte, cappuccino, macchiato; my dad'd think it's the Mafia. You a student?

RORY. Catering college. Wankshire. I knew most of it before I got there.

KEN. They must teach you *something*.

RORY. Yeah. How to turn on the cooker. Dad sent me for my own good. *His* good rather. He can't cook nothin'. Rubbery omelettes. Since Mam died it's me cookin' every day. 'cept I'm in deep doodoo. I made us onion soup. Well, I thought they were onions, his prize Daffodil bulbs. He should'na left 'em in the kitchen.

KEN. May I ask, have you run away from home?

RORY. Left. Left home. Dad's dip-stick. Granddad's all right, biding his time, though. Sent him home to die in my room. I'm in next door.

KEN. The dealer?

RORY. Two in a single bed. Plus he's crankin' one off three times a night watching Superman.

KEN. Superman?

RORY. The porn version.

KEN. Superman porn? I've never heard the like.

RORY. You need to get out more. Superman flies around Manhattan, dives into bedrooms for a quickie...

Moral of the story, shut the fuckin' winder. He's bi, actually.

KEN. Superman's bisexual? Gotham and Gomorrah!

RORY. Gay inclusive.

KEN. Now I've heard it all!

RORY. In tights an' all. It's not a fuckin' ballet, is it?

KEN. Talking technical, you need aerodynamic tights. You can't fly in a suit! *(Looking around.)* Mind what we say in 'ere.

RORY. Cameras can't *hear* as well, can they?

KEN. You're half my age. Keep talking.

RORY. OK, er... Them electric car chargers, I reckon they're killer robots from Planet Zog.

KEN. You don't say.

RORY. Lining up to invade Earth.

KEN. I hope you're wrong. I've no wish to be throttled by a malevolent charging cable. How many out there?

RORY. Joke, mister! There's no such place as Planet Zog.

KEN. I think I get that.

*(**KEN** is scanning the building.)*

RORY. Spiderman's got a girlfriend as well, but I dig the way he spins webs round the baddies.

KEN. Guy over there, look. The hoody. Flex-glow trainers, burger and fries, gallon of fizz, and a bag of jelly beans.

RORY. Blow out time, innit? You pay for all that ice.

KEN. Where *do* they get the money?

(They watch him pass by.)

RORY. I know what some of 'em do for cash. *(Sotto voce.)* Or maybe you don't wanna know. *(Money gesture, rubbing his fingers.)* You need a lift? Get out there and look sexy. The priest who dropped me off 'ere. First thing he says "How much?"

KEN. A priest?

RORY. A priest yeah. Dog collar, crucifix, all the kit. Ugly as a slug. Thought I'm a squaddie.

KEN. A priest cruising the M6 for squaddies. What's the world coming to?

RORY. Squaddies happy, cruisers happy, no problem.

KEN. Prostitution is no longer an offence, but kerb crawling is. They'll get him. Randy old bugger. I bet he's not the only one.

RORY. I told 'im, I'm straight.

KEN. Most squaddies *are* straight.

RORY. Gay for pay!

KEN. In this weather? How do they get it up?

RORY. They don't have to. You pay up front.

KEN. *(Pause.) You* seem to know.

RORY. Army pays peanuts. They still come in 'ere hungry, can't afford it like me...

KEN. Can I see your ID?

RORY. I'm nineteen.

KEN. Please show me your ID.

RORY. I'm an adult! Nineteen! I've got me passport.

> (**RORY** *digs into his rucksack for his passport.)*

You're not allowed to grow up in this country. You need ID to cross the fuckin' road.

KEN. You followed me from the slot machines to the toilets, and followed me out carrying a placard. Obviously, I'm not family. Blackpool, what for holiday?

RORY. New job. Can you take me all the way?

KEN. If I've enough juice to get there and back.

RORY. Near the gay village. A mate lives there, but he's in hospital. I need the key to his flat. Silly sod got run over crossing the road.

KEN. Looking at his mobile?

RORY. Crotch watching.

(*Shows his passport. Page open.*)

KEN. Don't the kids go down to Manchester these days? Half an hour on the train. It's jumpin' there, like London – so they say.

(**KEN** *gives the passport back.*)

Pretty as Batman's bum boy.

RORY. Not Batman please. Face like a brick.

KEN. What work d'you do?

RORY. Cheffin'. Interview tomorrow. Just got my hygiene certificate.

KEN. Well, that qualifies you to mop floors. Congratulations. Cooking what? Burgers, steaks, pizzas, Michelin star?

RORY. Head chef. Pub where my pal works.

KEN. Pub chef? You went to catering college to make a ploughman's?

RORY. Roast beef, shepherd's pie, rhubarb crumble. The buying, storage, cooking.

KEN. Pub's don't have head chefs.

RORY. This one does. Fifty covers lunch and dinner.

KEN. At nineteen?

RORY. Why not?

KEN. D'you know what? I reckon you're up to no good. Hanging around the toilets, chatting up blokes. You're soliciting. Doing your squaddie number, dressed for the part, asking me for money.

RORY. When?

KEN. Chicken bucket you said.

RORY. Hold on, mate. That's not askin' for money.

KEN. The warm up, and what comes next? *(Making to go.)* I know the game, sonny boy. I meet a lot of lads like you, sleepin' around. I wouldn't touch 'em with double condoms, plastic gloves and a face mask.

RORY. I'm after a fuck, not my appendix out.

KEN. I never pay for it. So, on your way, fellah. Stay out of trouble.

> *(**KEN** marches off.)*

RORY. Excuse me, Mister, respect? Fuckin' nutter.

> *(**RORY** retrieves his placard from the bin. Back at the table, he cautiously pops a red pill and washes it down with the latte. He hesitates and takes another one. Dials on his mobile.)*

(Phone call.) You awake? – I know you don't phone in your sleep, y'twat! And – I'm runnin' late, M6 somewhere. Dude offers me a lift then fucks off. Quite nice looking but mental. Full-on paranoia. Thinks he's being watched – I *am* careful. I don't do weird – Weirdos? Well, we know what you like, Hannibal Lecter. Anyway, this one only talks about money. Must be a Tory. How's your leg? – *Two* fractures? You don't do things by halves then? – Yep, Red Bomber, new

stuff, my dealer – a lot stronger than paracetamol. They turn you on like double strength Viagra. So only take one. One red bomber keeps you goin' all night. Hide them or they'll report you – doesn't matter how nice they are, stupid. It's their job; like what about other patients? – *they* care about them – hide them or you'll start an orgy in the ward – soon as I can. I swear you'll be pain-free in five minutes. Remember no more than one – I know I'm not your mother. Go back to sleep. I'll text you.

(**KEN** *returns.*)

(Call ends.) I thought you'd gone Mister.

KEN. *(They shake hands.)* Ken. Car's ready. It'll get me to Blackpool and back. Who was that?

RORY. *(Beat.)* Blackpool. Leg broke in two places. He's waiting for me.

KEN. Come on then. *(Beat.)* Yes? No?

RORY. Mister... I've gotta say it, I'm not rent.

KEN. Well, the way you were talking... I apologise. C'mon! Move!

(*Fist bump.*)

RORY. Safe.

(**RORY** *bins the placard.*)

(**RORY** *grabs his things. Follows* **KEN** *to the car park.*)

End of Scene One

(Sound effect: Car journey.)

Scene Two
Ken's house on the Moors
The living room

(The walls are bare. All the pictures, mirrors etc. have been removed. Ken's travel bags are on the floor.)

*(**RORY** is half-awake but sluggish in an armchair, still wearing his camo jacket and beanie. His rucksack is nearby.)*

*(**KEN** enters carrying a mug of tea. He puts the tea down, feels **RORY**'s forehead, whips off the beanie.)*

*(**RORY** groans.)*

KEN. Weak tea. Settle your stomach.

*(**KEN** looks around the bare room in disbelief.)*

Can you hear me? Drink your tea. Roy!

RORY. Rory. This is an empty house.

KEN. I've been burgled. I can't call the police, not with you here.

RORY. Why not?

KEN. Drugs. "Sir, what is your relationship with this young man?" Get it?

RORY. What drugs?

KEN. Your antics in the car, you've gotta be on *something*. Drink your tea.

RORY. I don't drink tea.

KEN. Sorry, we don't do latte.

RORY. I don't *like* tea.

KEN. Everybody likes tea.

RORY. *(Sitting up.)* Why've you brought me here?

KEN. Don't look so worried. I'm moving in. While I was in Manchester the place was robbed. All the antiques my dad left to me. Stuff I've known all my life.

RORY. Will you get it back?

KEN. Oh yes. I know who it is, family. Ivy, my dad's sister. Greedy old witch. Why do old people want more possessions? Don't stand up, she'll grab the cushion you're sat on.

RORY. Blimey!

KEN. I never call her aunty. I can't stand her. It's not nice to wish people dead, but...

RORY. You're lucky. My dad's got nothing to leave me.

KEN. They've no children to leave it to. Platonic love if you believe that. Meaning sex is purely for breeding purposes. *(Looking around.)* Even my dad's books have gone. Dad read a lot before B.V. Before vodka. Neat vodka, shot his liver to buggery. Nothing left but his clothes. If I take you to Blackpool I might drop his suits at a charity shop.

RORY. If? You promised me.

KEN. I know, but I didn't swear an affidavit. OK, I'll take you. I <u>will</u> take you if you stop...

RORY. What.

KEN. I'm talking about your conduct in the car. Need I spell it out? A fuckin' blow-job at seventy miles an hour?

RORY. Eh, charity shops. I know where the Heart Foundation is.

KEN. He died of liver –

RORY. When you die your heart stops. Can we go now?

KEN. Not yet. You've been comatose for two hours. Plus a high temperature, and a heart-rate faster than a Pixie's wank. I'm giving you a lift, not intensive care. That latte, what was in it? Answer please.

RORY. I'm knackered, aren't I? I walked a long way.

KEN. A priest picked you up.

RORY. An' dumped me, right? I walked for miles in the rain.

KEN. Listen, I'd to turn off the M6. You got over excited? That's the polite version. Put another way, you jumped on me like a dog on heat with two dicks.

RORY. I couldn't bloody find it, y'ten button jeans!

KEN. Listen, sunshine, the seat belt not only protects the passenger. It also protects the driver from sexual assault, notwithstanding face recognition.

RORY. No worries. You're quite nice looking – in a way.

KEN. Speed cameras. Motorway speed cameras every two-hundred metres. And now with Articial Intelligence they can see the colour of your eyes. They've got drones with cameras.

RORY. For your number plate.

KEN. And any hanky panky.

RORY. Cameras in the fuckin' sky? You're losing it, mate.

KEN. My picture with your head in my lap is now going viral round every police station in Greater Manchester, Lancashire, and Yorkshire. Oh, before we leave by the scenic route, you can sew my fly buttons back on. *(Beat.)* Are you receiving me?

RORY. This gets worser and worser. I've no time for this shit. I'm late.

KEN. I need to know what you're on.

RORY. Nowt! I'm on nowt. I told you I'm tired. Let's go please.

KEN. Sorry. I make the rules. You will do as I tell you.

RORY. I'm not into sub-dom. Jesus, it's cold in 'ere.

(**KEN** *shuts the window.*)

KEN. That better? You had a temperature of a hundred and two. I brought you here. I'm responsible for your welfare.

RORY. This is fuckin' manic, mister. You're making me jumpy.

KEN. Don't be, let's discuss the situation calmly. First question, are you back on planet Earth?

RORY. (*Sniggers.*) Oh, come on! Is this real for fuck's sake! OK, I'll make my own way back. Sorry, mate. I'm out of time. Have a nice day.

(**RORY** *stands up, but he's giddy and stumbles.*)

Shit, that latte's strong.

KEN. D'you mean what's in it?

RORY. Just a minute. I might be allergic to caffeine.

KEN. Sit down. Breathe in and out slowly, like meditation. Do it now. You're losing your balance. Don't add concussion to the list.

(**KEN** *makes him sit down.*)

RORY. That is an assault.

KEN. Technical assault, you're not hurt, and who y'gonna tell. Less of your cheek. Breathe deeply. Oxygen is a wonderful thing.

(**RORY** *breathes deeply but has a coughing fit. He drinks some tea.*)

RORY. It's like the Psycho house!

KEN. The mad house? Have you been there?

RORY. Anthony Perkins. Psycho! I've got the series. If you were taller, thinner and better looking, you could pass for Anthony Perkins.

KEN. Is that your idea of a compliment?

RORY. Anthony Perkins is a bit of alright.

KEN. He's dead.

> (**RORY** *rises again and staggers towards the exit in a fit of fear.*)

What's up now?

RORY. I'd better get going.

KEN. Not round 'ere. They all go to bed at nine o'clock.

RORY. I always get a lift.

KEN. You're not going nowhere. You can't even walk properly. I daren't call an ambulance. They also ask awkward questions.

RORY. Not if I'm not here.

KEN. Do as you're told! Sit down. I'll get you to Blackpool safely. This is not my fault. You followed me, remember? I did not follow you.

RORY. *(Sits down.)* I thought you fancied me.

KEN. Well, I also feel differently now. You're a vulnerable young drug addict.

RORY. Are you a social worker?

KEN. What are you on? Class A? Or class B? Street name crack? Spice? Crystal meth? What do <u>you</u> call it? Ice? Glass? *(In a bit of a temper.)* Oh, for God's sake pull yourself together. You haven't got the time? Neither have I.

RORY. Wind your neck in. You're fuckin' hang-ups. I'm not a crack'ead.

KEN. It's too late to drive to Blackpool. You haven't got the flat key. Where y'gonna stay?

RORY. I'll sleep under a pier.

KEN. The tide comes in. You might drown.

RORY. I'll find somewhere. I know Blackpool. I worked there last summer.

KEN. He says, like butter wouldn't melt in his mouth. Butter wouldn't melt if it slid right through you and dropped out your arse. It's me you're talking to, Sonny. So, I'll ask you again. What are you on? So I can deal with it in the proper manner, in case you have another episode. Hallucinations.

RORY. Mister, this is false imprisonment.

KEN. No, it's real imprisonment.

RORY. I know the law.

KEN. Know the law? In your state you couldn't piss your own initials in the snow.

RORY. I'll be OK by the time I get there.

KEN. It's twenty-miles back to the M6. In this weather you'll catch your death. The worst summer since records began.

(**KEN** *moves closer to* **RORY**.)

Watch my lips. Sober up. Then we'll go.

RORY. Don't look at me like that. You gimme the creeps.

KEN. No worries. It's the Lancashire Moors, but I'm no Ian Brady.

RORY. You're creepy enough. The moors murders? Myra Hindley and Ian Brady? That's all I fuckin' need.

KEN. I'm not creepy. It's all in your mind! Why I say get sober! Don't call me creepy!

RORY. Geeky then.

KEN. Oh, geeky now. What does that mean. Geeky.

RORY. I don't know! Just geeky. OK, not geeky, I take it back.

KEN. You can't unsay geeky.

RORY. Listen, my mobile can be traced.

KEN. I know that. Technology let's all hackers in. And they all think they're experts in crime management. So, who's looking for you?

RORY. My friend in Blackpool if I don't turn up.

KEN. Are you officially a missing person? Please establish your exact whereabouts on your phone. Then tell your friend you're on your way.

(**RORY** *looks up his location.*)

You got yourself into this situation. Don't blame me. I was just having a break. I wasn't expecting to meet the son of Satan. Go on. Tell your friend where you are.

RORY. You don't own me. You don't decide my life.

KEN. No, but I decide mine. We're gonna do this carefully and slip into Blackpool unnoticed.

RORY. All I want is to get there. Fuck, I wish I were there now.

KEN. So do I.

RORY. Instead of kidnapped by a fuckin' geek.

KEN. What's a geek? I'm dying to know.

RORY. I'm due in Blackpool! That's it! End of!

KEN. With brain fog. A job interview in your condition?

RORY. *(Mobile location.)* Shit, we're no nearer Blackpool. We've gone South.

KEN. East. I told you, the Lancashire Moors. You're my first visitor. Let's celebrate.

RORY. I thought you weren't in the mood.

KEN. Tea and biscuits.

RORY. *(Finds his exact location.)* Saddleworth! Saddleworth Moor? Where the bodies were buried!

KEN. Sixty-years-ago. People still do walking tours of the graves, rather distasteful in my opinion. They all say they study criminology. Ho ho. You don't learn much staring at the grass.

RORY. Geeky, see? *They're* geeks! It's what I'm sayin'. Geeks, weirdos!

KEN. Like me? I may lose my job for this. Trapped in your sordid little world of sex, drugs and rent boys. You're a bad influence on your generation and you don't care.

RORY. I'm not any of that. I'm just me.

KEN. Drug addicts only care about their next hit.

RORY. Are you talking to me? Listen, mate, you owe me.

KEN. Geek, is that the latest drug? Never mind, I'll Google it. Meantime, I'm obliged to inform you about S.U.D. Substance Use Disorder, moderate or severe.

RORY. You're a youth worker.

KEN. Drugs alter perception, ghosts, aliens from outer space, and whatever geeks are.

(**KEN** *looks up geeky on his mobile.*)

RORY. You talk shit like a youth worker.

KEN. Oh, so you know. OK, geek. "A person who is socially inept or clumsy. A person obsessed with technology.

A fairground performer whose act consists of bizarre tricks like swallowing live frogs, or biting the heads off live chickens." *(Shuts down his mobile.)* So, which am I? Live frogs or chickens?

(**RORY** *buries his face in his hands.*)

What's the matter now?

RORY. Please God, make him leave me alone! I never said you eat live frogs! You're giving me a headache!

KEN. You got your own headache. Look at me. You're coming down from summat nasty. Dilated pupils. Eyes like a demented meerkat. We'll leave when you're sober. I mean that. When you're sober.

RORY. *(Weary.)* How masterful, I love it. What's the time now?

KEN. On your watch or mine?

(*They look at their watches.*)

You don't realise. If I were stopped swerving across lanes with you in the car... high detectability breathalizers... I lose my license.

RORY. We didn't do anything.

KEN. I might as well tell you. I'm on extended sick leave, in other words suspended. I might get away with careless driving on my own. But not with a passenger.

RORY. We didn't do anything. I'm just sayin'.

KEN. My quick thinking got us off the motorway. What else could I do? Chuck you out in the rain?

RORY. I'm just sayin'. We did nowt wrong. Ken, I'm just sayin'.

KEN. Stop sayin' *you're just sayin'*, allow me to say. Drug abuse: I do know the signs. I'm practised in first aid. However, in the interests of due diligence, I am consulting the sacred oracle, Google again.

RORY. Jesus.

KEN. Update. Crystal meth side effects.

RORY. It's not crystal meth.

KEN. Ah! We have a confession. I dare say the side effects are similar. Nausea, giddiness, confusion, fast pulse-rate, slow pulse-rate, hallucinations, hyperactivity, all at the same time. Add to which, a juvenile mentality. And these hallucinations, like the ghost you saw on the stairs...

RORY. A ghost? When?

KEN. The old man on the stairs.

RORY. No, that was real.

KEN. There's no such thing as ghosts. An old man in pyjamas? Pull the other one. Certainly not my dad. He never wore pyjamas.

RORY. It was an old geyser in pyjamas. Snoopy pattern.

KEN. Obviously you want Snoopy pyjamas for Christmas.

RORY. No no, you're quite wrong. Spiderman.

KEN. Look, I don't believe in life after death. Eternal life for pyjamas? Not even Marks & Spencers say their pyjamas are that good. D'you remember anything of what's actually happened?

RORY. No worries. You're gorgeous. Defo. What about a kiss?

KEN. Let me check your pulse again. Roy, I am formally asking your permission to check your pulse.

RORY. Why bother asking?

KEN. Correct procedure. Pulse please.

RORY. Are we playing naughty doctors? Things are lookin' up.

KEN. Pulse! I'm practised in first aid. Part of my job. Sit still. *(Takes pulse.)*

KEN. Can you stand up yet? Try again.

RORY. Don't be such a twat.

KEN. Stand up! I have the power to make you comply if you don't co-operate.

RORY. Manic. I'm not into S&M.

> *(Pause. **RORY** stands up cautiously.)*

KEN. Now walk towards me in a straight line. In a straight line please.

RORY. Is this what you have to do round 'ere for a fuck?

KEN. Walk towards me.

> *(**RORY** walks, arms stretched like a tightrope walker.)*

Keep going, keep going…

RORY. Mister, it's not the fuckin' circus. *(**RORY** does his best.)* All good, see?

KEN. Stand on one leg.

RORY. Like a stork?

KEN. On one leg! Can you balance?

RORY. *This* is geeky. Hear what I say? Fuckin' geeky as Hell. OK, watch me.

> *(**RORY** balances on one leg.)*

KEN. How's your breathing now?

> *(**RORY** collapses. **KEN** catches him and guides him back to the chair.)*

Here's me stuck indoors with a teenage sex-maniac. If anyone says I should be so lucky, I'll fuckin' deck them.

> (**KEN** *takes his top off and grabs a sweater from his luggage.*)

In the morning, I'll do the decent thing and get you to Blackpool. What time is this bloody interview? I've work to do.

RORY. When did you stop going to the gym?

KEN. Don't be cheeky.

RORY. You need to work on that two-pack.

KEN. You could do worse.

RORY. Oh, are we on again?

> (**KEN** *puts his sweater on.*)

I'll make you up a bed for tonight. At least they haven't stolen the bed linen.

RORY. On my own? Oh, it's off again.

KEN. Six bedrooms, take your pick.

RORY. Is this what they call psychological torture? Your kitchen's a shock to the system. I've never seen anything like it. Who does the washing up round 'ere? Anyone?

KEN. What were you doing in the kitchen?

RORY. Water, after I was sick.

KEN. Or more drugs? Don't do this to me.

RORY. Water! Dirty glass an' all.

KEN. I know what it's like. I haven't had a chance. My dad lived on his own. He couldn't do anything for himself.

RORY. There's a dead mouse in a pan of gravy.

KEN. It's a sausage.

RORY. With a tail?

KEN. Hallucinating.

RORY. Cockroaches in a sardine tin.

KEN. Nope. No cockroaches.

RORY. I know what a cockroach is. I've worked in enough restaurants. Can't we leave now? It's me job, Ken. Me Dad'll kill me if I lose *this* one.

KEN. *This* one?

> (**KEN** *taps in a number on his mobile.*)

RORY. *(Rises from his seat.)* I'm OK now, look.

KEN. Just a minute. *(Phone.)* Ivy, listen carefully. Listen *very* carefully to this message. I got back tonight to find the house has been stripped of valuables. You have no legal right to be in possession of the keys. Why take so much? Are you opening an antique shop? Take due note. You must return all dad's property now, all of it, the clock, the pictures, antiques. They're worth folding money. The paintings and my *Dad's Army* picture. It's quite simple. I want my childhood memories back. It's just like the solicitor said. After the funeral, that's when the fun starts. But you won't have much fun in court, or with your name in the papers. If you don't answer the door to the police, they'll use a battering ram. I'll make sure of that.

> (**RORY** *quietly collects his things and sidles towards the door.*)

Oi! Where d'you think you're goin'? *(Closes the call.)*

The doors are locked.

RORY. I'm trapped!

KEN. Apprehended.

RORY. *(With his mobile ready.)* Ken, if you're not gonna fuck me, this is kidnapping. I'll call the police.

KEN. I am the police.

RORY. Shit!

End of Scene Two

Scene Three
Next day, nine a.m.

(**IVY** *is sitting in a chair, a Victorian walking stick propped up beside her. On the floor, boxes of stolen items.*)

(**KEN** *enters carrying another box. He puts it with the others.*)

KEN. A few mementos? You took it all! Three floors. What d'you think you're doing? Ivy, this is organised crime. Headline: Bonnie and Clyde on tonic wine...

IVY. My own brother. Don't I get anything?

KEN. The medals, me dad's medals? And I'll have that walking stick. It belonged to Queen Victoria.

IVY. Who told you that?

KEN. Dad. He was proud of it.

IVY. Queen Victoria? Huh. I'd take that with a *very* large pinch of salt. Five years ago you left! We thought we'd never see you again. Especially under the circumstances.

KEN. Five years isn't long for a family feud. They can last for generations.

IVY. Are you still suffering from depression?

KEN. I'll ignore that remark for the sake of goodwill.

IVY. Kenneth, we never thought you'd be back. No word for years! No messages. No phone calls. Not even a postcard. How could anyone know? We thought you'd gone to live abroad.

KEN. Or you hoped I had. I haven't left the force. I was never far away. The medals please.

IVY. Why? They're no use to you.

KEN. Or you. It's all what's left of the old bugger. You obviously know where they are.

IVY. I don't know. Derek did it all.

KEN. Oh, your wheelman.

IVY. What?

KEN. Y'getaway car. Derek won't want his name in the papers either. Not Alderman Derek.

IVY. Leave Derek out of it.

KEN. You're the brains.

IVY. Stop tormenting us. We've done nowt wrong. You can't leave an empty house full of antiques. Please be reasonable.

KEN. That car is an Aladdin's cave on wheels. In law, Derek's as guilty as you are. As an accomplice. He shut the car window in my face. I wonder why.

IVY. Haven't you noticed? It's raining! He won't be long.

KEN. Dad only died a month ago. What about probate?

IVY. Probate don't know where things are. It's just paperwork. He'd been dead a month when I found him. You've no idea what it was like.

KEN. Why did you leave him that long?

IVY. We were on holiday.

(**KEN** *begins to open the boxes.*)

It's not stealing if it's family. Ask any judge.

KEN. Be aware that stealing from family is an offence.

IVY. Kenneth. I came here in peace. You haven't even offered me a cup of tea.

KEN. There isn't any.

IVY. *(Points to the empty tea mug on the table.)* Who's had that then?

KEN. Damn, those mice again. Look at this stuff. You strolled in, helped yourselves, and drove off with two car loads.

IVY. I'm entitled to something of sentimental value.

KEN. You'll be lucky if you get a mustard spoon. It's polite to ask first. But *don't* ask me now. A refusal may cause offence. Here's me teaching the elderly good manners.

> (**KEN** *takes some of the antiques out of the boxes and places them around the room or on the floor.)*

IVY. I was born in this house. Surely I'm entitled to what's mine.

KEN. Nothing's yours.

IVY. You've no consideration. I bought some of those things. Ask Derek. Derek knows the law.

KEN. Oh, now Derek know the law. Why does everybody think they know the law? Derek has two brain cells which don't function at the same time.

IVY. Have y'done? Have y'done with sarcasm? Your father's turning in his grave.

KEN. I believe he was cremated.

IVY. He'd be turning in his grave if he had one. He wouldn't want all this bad blood between us.

KEN. You started it.

IVY. You disappeared without a trace.

KEN. Doesn't alter the facts. I am the sole inheritor. Me, myself and I. No arguments. End of.

IVY. If you mean beneficiary...and only on paper.

KEN. What d'you mean only on paper? D'you own *your* house only on paper? How d'you think I felt when I came in and saw these bare walls?

IVY. You never used to be like this.

KEN. The Will is crystal clear. My house and all its contents, whatsoever they may be, wheresoever they may be situate.

IVY. Solicitor's jargon. There's also moral considerations.

KEN. I'm asking for what's right. My bloody property, have you've still got it all. *(Beat.)* Have you still got it all? For a start, what about the clock?

IVY. I refuse to discuss this further until you modify your tone.

KEN. I *have* modified my tone. You'd be green, blue and purple by now if I hadn't.

IVY. I'm not frightened of you Kenneth. And you're all talk by the way. That's a sign of weakness.

KEN. I still want the clock.

IVY. Why?

KEN. I don't know why. It's alway been there.

IVY. It's not all that valuable.

KEN. It's gold-plated.

IVY. Gold leaf.

KEN. You're hedging. You've sold it? If you've sold that clock, I'll find it, if I have to scour every antique shop and auction in the county.

IVY. He *gave* me the clock! That's why I'm keeping it.

KEN. I've only got your word for it.

IVY. You're not getting the clock!

>   (**KEN** *goes back to the boxes. He finds the framed photo.)*

KEN. Lake Windermere.

(*He places it on the mantelpiece.*)

IVY. I wanted to keep that. I'm on it.

KEN. This room without it is like a picnic without scenery. Can't you see what matters? How he was before...

IVY. Of course I remember Lake Windermere. The paddle steamer. We all went on it together, didn't we? All round the Lake and then a cream tea. There's more pictures upstairs the bedrooms.

KEN. Bedrooms. You did a full clearance, eh? Thanks for leaving me something to sleep on.

(**KEN** *puts the photo above the fireplace.*)

IVY. Oh, give over. Why would we take the beds?

KEN. You would if you could carry them.

IVY. Kenneth what's happened to you? Every word you say is so offensive. Every single word. But you've got it all wrong. You're wrong and we all know why, don't we? We all know, Kenneth. Your paranoia! You see the worst in everyone.

KEN. There's always the worst.

IVY. All I can say is this. I did not set you and your father apart. I did not tell him you're a homosexual. He worked it out for himself. You're late thirties and unmarried. Long term depression.

KEN. You poisoned his mind with snide comments. Are yer courting yet? If not, why not? Every time you came through that door. Every bloody time.

IVY. It was a jest, Kenneth. Everyone says it.

KEN. Say it enough times folk cotton on. You had an agenda, to get this property. My own father calls me the runt in a litter of one, and orders me out of the house. I believe you were present at the time.

IVY. No. You walked out. You're too temperamental, Kenneth. Too temperamental by far. You bear grudges.

KEN. Good for the soul.

IVY. You walked out with two suitcases, a taxi waiting.

(*Silence as* **KEN** *takes more objects out of boxes.*)

If that's what I said too many times, Kenneth, I'm sorry. I didn't mean it that way. There is such a thing as forgiveness. Forgive and forget. Can we do that please? You've got what you want.

KEN. Typical Ivy. Big on morality. Low on morals. How does it go? Dad told me when you lived in Manchester, Derek came home early and found you on the parlour floor with a six-foot-six brickie.

IVY. I beg your pardon!

KEN. Back in the day. Flighty, Dad said. Mini skirts up to here. Is it true you wore stilettoes on the beach?

IVY. Don't be so bloody daft. He was kidding you. He was kidding you, Kenneth! Anyway, all the girls wore mini-skirts. They still do, don't they? D'you know, Kenneth, I'm stunned the things you say to me! Stilettoes on the beach? Bonny and Clyde? Are you making it up? I'm absolutely stunned!

KEN. Ivy, they couldn't stun you in the electric chair.

IVY. Right! If *you're* so respectable, who's that young lad upstairs looking out the window? Mmmm? I think I know why he's here. I'm not blinkered. Where did you find him?

KEN. None of your business.

IVY. How old is he?

KEN. Nineteen. I'm giving him a lift to Blackpool. He was stranded on the motorway in the rain.

IVY. You've changed a lot. I'm seeing another side of you and I don't much like it.

KEN. *(Flips.)* OK, That's it! Gimme the house keys and go. Now please, the keys. From now on, no one enters this house without my permission.

IVY. *(Staying put.)* I shall wait for Derek.

KEN. I'll get you a cab.

IVY. Don't bother. I won't get into it. I shan't be ejected from the house where I was born. Where are your manners?

KEN. If I fetch up in your house when it suits me, I'd like to hear what you say.

IVY. You heard me.

KEN. Am I right, or am I right?

IVY. The family home? I'm not allowed in?

KEN. Ivy, we are where we are. I don't like you, you don't like me. Call it a day. *(Takes out his mobile.)* I didn't want to do this. I was going to spare you the embarrassment. Take a look. A little video show. You're the star. A bit fuzzy, but we can see it's you.

IVY. What?

KEN. New security camera. Installed last week. Here we go.

(**KEN** *plays the video. Shows it to* **IVY**.)

That's you and Derek red-handed. Your car, primary evidence. There you both are carrying bagfuls and boxes.

IVY. That is despicable.

KEN. That's what I thought.

IVY. Doing that to us.

KEN. After this, we move on with our separate lives, don't we? Nuff sai–?

IVY. How sad. How sad, Kenneth, that you resort to spying on your family.

KEN. How did I know? Forgive and forget? There's no way back from this.

IVY. We shall say a prayer for you. Who knows if the good Lord will hear us. Blessed are the peacemakers, for they shall be called sons of God. Blessed are the meek, for they shall inherit the Earth.

KEN. Everyone wants to rule the world, these days, even the fuckin' meek.

(**IVY** *circles the room, using the walking stick.*)

(**RORY** *enters discreetly and waits in the doorway. They don't see him.*)

IVY. Your father's not dead. He's fallen asleep in the peace of God. He was so ill at the end. Acute chest pain. We called an ambulance but he refused it. Adamant, no hospitals. The ambulance crew did their best to persuade him, but he'd made up his mind. Enough was enough. Wouldn't let her in. Made an awful fuss about it. She was born here, actually. But that didn't cut much ice, ranting and raving. Derek and me, we didn't know where to put ourselves. Good job, she accepted our apology. But she had the last word: for every bigot who dies another one is born.

KEN. C'est la vie.

IVY. Are you gonna sell? I hope you're not a drinker. You don't want to turn into your father. In the end, *he* gave up on the world. Hardly ever went out. Eventually, he never went out at all. Had the vodka delivered to the door. He slept in his clothes. Slept in his boots. The dog found a sack of food in the kitchen and drank water out of the toilet. The chaise longue was in a right mess. We had to burn it. As for the booze! Vodka for breakfast, vodka for lunch, vodka for tea. We found him on the chaise longue lying in his own mess.

RORY. What sort of dog?

KEN. *(To* **RORY.***)* Shove off. There's a good lad.

RORY. There's no time, Ken!

KEN. Two minutes! Go on!

IVY. We got him into a hospice.

KEN. *(Shoos* **RORY** *out.)* Get cleaned up for the interview. *(To* **IVY.***)* He wants his breakfast. We're off to Blackpool. Job interview.

IVY. Who is he?

KEN. Ivy, let it rest. I don't know him. He's a hitchhiker.

IVY. I was born in this house, and now I leave it disposessed.

KEN. One more thing. Where *is* Bobby? *(Beat.)* No answer. I'll try again. What's happened to Bobby?

IVY. He couldn't manage a dog.

KEN. So, what happened? I said what happened!

IVY. Don't shout! I had nothing to do with it.

KEN. Nothing to do with what? Bobby was a happy dog. What happened? You got rid of him?

IVY. I wasn't involved! That's all I'm saying.

KEN. If you knew about it, you were involved. Was he let loose on the moors to fend for himself? Or worse, put down. Was he euthanised?

IVY. Some things are for the best.

KEN. Best for who?

IVY. We had no choice.

>   *(Pause.)*

You left Bobby behind. Why?

KEN. Dad loved him as well. He needed him.

IVY. The Prodigal Son returns, expects it all ticketyboo, as if nothing's happened.

KEN. Prodigal Son? No, I'm Abomination according to St. Paul. Mind you, he wasn't a Saint at the time.

IVY. You believed in the Bible once. What went wrong?

KEN. I read it. Well, the bits they made movies of.

RORY. *(Offstage.)* Ken! Ken! Where are me jeans! Me jeans, Ken!

KEN. *(To **IVY**.)* Excuse me.

>   *(**KEN** exits to go upstairs. **IVY** scurries to the door and calls after him.)*

>   *(Derek's car draw up.)*

IVY. You don't know what it was like! You've no idea! Waltzing back in here like the Lord of the Manor! Bobby was your responsibility!

>   *(She takes the house keys out of her bag and slams them down on the coffee table. Then snatches the picture of her brother from the mantelpiece.)*

My brother! Keep the damn keys!

>   *(She scurries out to the car, leaving her walking stick behind. Door slams.)*

End of Scene Three

Scene Four

(**RORY** *is lying on the sofa. He is wearing one of Ken's football T-shirts, boxer shorts and white socks.*)

(*There is a folding stepladder near the window.* **KEN** *enters carrying clean jeans, T-shirt, and a glass of water. He puts the water down.*)

RORY. Is that a clean glass?

KEN. Shut up. I've only got paracetamol. Don't you dare take anything stronger. If you were a few years younger I'd be ringing your Father. Here look, your clean vest.

RORY. I like this one, the colour.

KEN. Drink plenty of water, you're dehydrated. (*Puts it down.*)

RORY. Can I keep this?

KEN. Drink it. Rory, It's a known fact, if you don't drink enough fluid, your dick shrinks.

　　　　(**RORY** *sits up.*)

Works every time. How's your head?

　　　　(**RORY** *drinks some water.*)

RORY. So, if I drink six pints a day will it grow bigger?

KEN. Ask the tooth fairy. (*Presents clean jeans.*) Put them on. You can't go for an interview in filthy jeans.

RORY. Has *her* gone, the witch.

KEN. (*Points to the walking stick.*) Yeah, but she forgot her walking stick. She'll be back for it, hopefully with the clock. Get dressed.

RORY. I feel like death.

KEN. Overdose. The fright you gave me. Don't die here. You'll overstay your welcome. Caught with a teenager on drugs is one thing. A dead teenager is more difficult to explain.

RORY. You're so nervy all the time. You're making *me* feel jumpy now.

KEN. *(Shoves the jeans at him.)* Put these on!

RORY. Yessir! Right away Sir! Take the fuckin' poker out yer arse, Ken chill!

KEN. Put them on.

RORY. Obviously. I'm not going to Blackpool in your running gear.

KEN. Boxing. It's a two-hour drive, and no funny business.

RORY. Boxing?

KEN. Did you hear me? No funny business.

RORY. Scout's honour. Like my Dad allus says. Scout's honour.

KEN. Taught you *some* decency then.

RORY. Nah, the dirty pig. Talks with his mouth full. Egg on his beard. Rice pudding's off limits defo. I refuse to make it. Never washes his hands either. I always know, cuz the toilets still flushing when he comes out. The sink's still dry and the hand towel hasn't been moved.

KEN. Get yer act together. Phone your mate. Blame the bad weather. Manchester's had the heaviest rainfall since records began. In Blackpool business is so slow the fish and chip shops are fuckin' suicidal.

> *(**RORY** takes off the T-shirt. **KEN** looks on. **RORY** notices **KEN**'s gaze. Sexual tension.)*

(**KEN** *snaps out of it and sits on the stepladder.*)

RORY. What's up?

KEN. Nothing.

RORY. I don't get many knock-backs.

KEN. Stand in the rain and cool off.

RORY. How old are you, Ken, Forty-five?

KEN. Forty-three. But only in daylight. Get dressed.

RORY. *(Headache.)* Erghhh!

KEN. Now what?

RORY. *(Head in hands.)* Headache. Shit! Gimme a paracetamol.

KEN. No way. I wouldn't trust you with M&Ms.

RORY. Flashes in my eyes. It's migraine.

KEN. Stop acting up.

RORY. I do get migraines.

KEN. I don't believe you.

(**RORY** *rushes to the window and draws the curtains.*)

What's all this?

RORY. I have to lie down in a dark room.

KEN. D'you take anything for it? No no, let's not go there.

(**RORY** *lies on the sofa.*)

You'd better not be having me on. I've had more fuckin' pandemonium than I can take in one day. You'll never get to Blackpool at this rate. Take a nap in the car. Rory!

RORY. What?

KEN. If the pain doesn't go away, I *will* have to call an ambulance. I'm obliged to. Don't put me in a difficult position. Remember we have not done anything. Don't start telling tales. That's nothing personal. It just isn't happening. The gay scene, it's not my style. It's for those who enjoy it, not me. I don't like crowds, I don't like discos.

RORY. D'you like happiness?

(*Silence.*)

Seeeeriously weeeeird!

KEN. When people suspect you're gay it's worse than if they know.

(**RORY** *sits bolt upright.*)

RORY. Are you still a virgin?

KEN. No comment.

RORY. Well, are you really a cop?

KEN. Suspended. I'm on a Disciplinary. After my workout, in the showers, this twat calls me a filthy faggot. "Eh, faggot! In other countries people like you are lined up against a wall and shot." I smacked him so hard he cut his head on the shower taps, burst a blood vessel, nearly scalped him, he collapsed on the tiles, blood everywhere, swirling down the plug-hole.

RORY. Like in Psycho?

KEN. Just like Psycho.

RORY. When Norman Bates slashes the woman in the shower, and the blood's going down the plug-hole. Classic. I've got 'em all. Psycho I, II, III, IV, and the remake. Anthony Perkins as Norman Bates, I wouldn't chuck him out of bed.

KEN. I know, you told me. If I was like Norman Bates, I'd be digging your grave by now.

RORY. What about the body parts in your freezer.

KEN. The freezer? You been down the cellar? I went to the supermarket while you were sleeping it off. Leg of lamb. Pork loin, topside.

RORY. Joke, y'daft bugger. My Dad can't take a joke either. Daffodil soup, he couldn't see the funny side. Tasted alright. I didn't tell him 'til he'd finished.

KEN. I feel sorry for your Dad.

RORY. I ought to feel sorry for him, but I don't. And to think I came into this world down his waste disposal unit. At least it was a short journey. That guy who called you a faggot. He deserved what he got.

KEN. It wasn't the real me. My boxing days suddenly zoomed back in, but I don't do drugs. You might get flashbacks though.

RORY. Were you professional?

KEN. Amateur fly weight. Won a few rounds.

RORY. Good for you, Ken I'm glad you did something good once.

KEN. Rory, I want you to understand. If I'm caught with you in my car, they'll throw the book at me. Unprofessional conduct, gross misconduct, inappropriate behaviour, gross indecency. That's why I'm waiting for you to come down from your bad trip. It's not kidnapping.

RORY. Will you get the sack?

KEN. And there's my pension to think about. Are you prepared for your interview?

RORY. *(Pause.)* It's not really an interview.

KEN. Another tall tale, is it?

RORY. Ken, don't go off on one!

KEN. Try me.

RORY. Well, it *is* a meeting. Where my mate works, the manager's giving me a job, no interview, no questions asked.

KEN. *(Clicks fingers.)* Just like that.

RORY. So, I thought that's a bit suspect. Sees my pictures and give me a job. I've *got* references. Maybe I shouldn't go.

KEN. They can't be expecting you anyway in this weather. By the way, while you're still here the house rules still apply. My rules. Get dressed anyway.

　　　　(Pause.)

RORY. That's what started it all. I'm making dinner, he goes up to his room to watch porn. He thinks I don't know. But on the quiet I'd turned on parental controls. He went mad. And when I said "your zip's still undone, y'mad wanker." He took his belt to me.

KEN. Illegal. Section 3 of the Domestic Abuse Act. But there's a shorter way. We knock on the door, rush him and give him a damn good thrashing. He won't do it again.

RORY. Can I watch?

KEN. Aw, c'mere, pal. I'm sorry.

　　　　*(**KEN** hugs **RORY**.)*

You're a little rascal, but deep down, you want to do good. Keep the T-shirt c'mon. *(Tenderly.)* OK, kid? *(Beat.)* Rory?

RORY. *(Beat.)* You feelin' a bit frisky?

KEN. *(Let's go of **RORY**.)* This is not just a bit of a high. It's the whole psychodynamic showcase. Eventually, drugs alter your brain patterns. I know that, you know that, we both know that's the truth. You've got to stop now before you end up on the streets. I'm not goin' off on one.

RORY. A quiet off on one.

KEN. One overdose can kill. Cardiac arrest.

RORY. When you're dead you don't know you're dead. I wouldn't wanna die in this dump. Why don't you paint it a happy colour, Primrose.

KEN. Maybe. This is a fine house in an area of outstanding natural beauty. It might make a nice B&B. It's not the Psycho House. Now, put all that scary stuff out of your mind. Do I look like a killer?

RORY. Killers don't look like killers. They're like you and me. Mostly you. Like you said, any stranger on a bus.

KEN. I've heard enough. Go upstairs and lie down.

RORY. Oh, are we back on?

KEN. In your dreams. *(Picks up the glass of water.)* Drink this first.

RORY. What is it?

KEN. Tap water.

RORY. Tap water from out there? That's a fuckin' aquarium, mate. Microbes, amoebas. See what I'm sayin'? It's infectious. Home-grown Covid. *(Puts the water down.)* I'm not drinking that!

KEN. What about the junk you put in *your* body? Orange juice then? It's fresh from the shop, unopened.

(Heads for the door to get it.)

RORY. Hold on! Where you keepin' it? That dirty fridge? Got any coke?

KEN. Which kind? No to both.

RORY. Sprite, 7-up, Dr. Pepper?

KEN. There's a mountain spring along the way. Pure water. If we had time, we could take a walk. Pity. I'll clean up the kitchen when I get back. I'm sorry it doesn't meet your high standards. Now, are you hungry yet? You should have the munchies by now. Want a doughnut? Clean doughnuts in a clean packet in a clean bag.

RORY. Ken, there's maggots in there.

KEN. White rice.

RORY. Rice don't wriggle.

KEN. It does when you're trippin'. Look who's talkin'. Just now you pissed out the window.

RORY. The toilet won't flush. I can't piss on other people's jobbies.

KEN. I think that hygiene certificate's gone to your head. Is it true, this hygiene qualification?

RORY. Yep. And two GCSEs.

KEN. What in? Wankin' n chillin'?

RORY. It's bad manners to jack off in a guestroom. If I wasn't locked in, I'd a done it in the garden.

KEN. I lock the doors at night. Doesn't every one? Get your kit together. Where's your mobile?

RORY. Upstairs. On the bed you left me to die on.

KEN. Excuse me, I may have saved your life. Cruising the M6 for guys is not the safest way to get around.

RORY. I don't do that!

KEN. You cruised me easy enough.

RORY. I don't even go out at nights. Only with the dog. That's the worst of it, leaving home. My dog. I can see her face now, waiting for me.

KEN. You don't go out at night, but you cruise the motorway.

RORY. I'm talking about my dog!

KEN. *(Rolls his eyes.)* Go on then, the dog.

RORY. One day I'll go back for her. I heard you talkin' about your dog. Did that old witch have it put down? I'd put <u>her</u> down.

KEN. If you miss the dog so much, why did you leave home?

RORY. I need a job. Lost my old job in a ruck with the boss. Zero hours, minimum wage. It's a fuckin' joke. Anyway, he's not a proper chef. Chicken shop franchise with a fuckin' frying pan.

KEN. Did y'dad really take his belt to you? Let me see you walk. You're limping.

(**RORY** *obediently walks back and forth.*)

You're limping. You may have had a stroke.

RORY. Pins and needles. I was lying on it! *(Flops down on the sofa.)* I can't handle this. Like the world's gone mad. I only stopped off for a quick piss. I just wanna see my dog. Fuck Blackpool. She's calling me.

KEN. What's her name?

RORY. Brindle! Brindle colour.

KEN. So you <u>call</u> her Brindle.

RORY. Fuck me, you're clever.

(**RORY** *gets dressed.*)

Young people don't have strokes.

(**KEN** *glances at* **RORY**. *Then studiously mounts the steps near the window to check the locks.*)

KEN. Don't be so sure. I've seen it all in my job. Young people on cannabis all day, they can get a stroke.

RORY. What yer doin' now? Aren't we goin'?

KEN. Window locks. Insurance.

RORY. Can't you do that later? Ken, when you stop playin' Spiderman...

KEN. I'm not dressing up as Spiderman. This lock's buggered. It's an open invitation.

(**KEN** *comes down off the steps.*)

Got any money left? Or did you spent it on happy pills?

RORY. I got no chance, have I? Not even with a deadbeat copper, acting like you're on duty and giving orders. You need help. I need something to eat.

(*Silence.* **RORY** *puts his trainers on.*)

KEN. Well get lunch on the motorway.

RORY. All-day breakfast?

KEN. If there's time.

(**KEN** *grabs Rory's bag and empties it on the sofa.*)

RORY. What the fuck... You're violating my privacy. Oi, that's my things! Have you got a search warrant?

(**KEN** *holds up a sachet.*)

KEN. Red Bombers? They ain't Smarties, are they? This lot? Dealers sell 'em one at a time. This is dealin'. You're dealin'! It's my duty to arrest you.

RORY. But you won't, because you kidnapped me, and ogling me inappropriately, thank God.

(*Pause.*)

KEN. No way do I take you to anywhere with this in my car. We get stopped and I'm done, and you're done.

RORY. Well, what we gonna do?

KEN. Down the road and chuck 'em over a hedge.

RORY. The cows are jumpin' over the moon. Ken. This is the truth. I told you I stayed next door; who's a supplier. He gave me them. You'll need something on a wet night like this, but only take one or you'll... My friend in Blackpool, he'll be disappointed, but...

KEN. I'm disappointed.

RORY. So, when I met you in the toilet I'm thinking my lucky day. Dick and dope together. But then you do sleazy talk like like your some hot shot porn star. Mister, you're family style! So don't kid yourself!

KEN. Sleazy? Not me. I don't do sleazy talk.

RORY. If *you* didn't say it, you've got the only talking dick on the planet. What about you, all that carry on about a fight. The guy in the shower, broke his jaw, burst a blood vessel, blood pouring down the plug'ole. Too much detail! When you put me in bed did you undress me, did you...?

KEN. Nope. I never touched you.

RORY. I know. You've got more morals than Mary Poppins.

> *(Sound of a car. **KEN** darts to the window to see who it is.)*

Is it the witch?

KEN. Something wicked this way comes.

RORY. Walt Disney. I've got it.

KEN. Shakespeare, actually, Macbeth.

> *(**KEN** grabs the walking stick.)*

RORY. Don't hit her, she's old!

>(**RORY** *wrenches the walking stick from* **KEN.**)

KEN. She's come back for it! I'm gonna give it to her!

RORY. Oh, no, Ken, no violence!

KEN. As a memento of my father! Lay off! She wants a memento. She can have one. This! Although, I could use it for burglars.

RORY. Get another one.

>(*Doorbell.*)

>(**KEN** *goes out to answer the door.*)

Get a dog! I would. My Brindle'd see 'em off! *(Sad.)* Brindle?

End of Scene Four

Scene Five

(KEN and IVY. She is wearing her coat, which she keeps on. She leans on the walking stick. The gilt clock is on the mantelpiece.)

(KEN opens the curtains and the clock glows in the sunlight.)

(Pause, as they gaze at it.)

KEN. *(Looking at his watch.)* I've got to top up the car.

IVY. Derek had already booked our flight. I phoned the District Nurse's office the minute we got here. What about his medication? This is criminal negligence! Oh, I gave them what for, I can assure you. How dare they leave a sick old man in such distress! He didn't know what tablets to take or when. He couldn't remember much. The doctor asked him his name. He remembered that. He asked him his date of birth. He could not remember that. But what the mind doesn't know, the heart still feels. Like the stars in the sky, which disappear in daylight, but they're still there, aren't they? Doctors don't think of things like that.

KEN. They're not in the church.

IVY. The hospice was more like a hotel. Not like the old days teeming with nuns. Beautiful garden! Hollyhocks and roses. Salmon and cucumber sandwiches. Macaroons! What a nice place to die.

KEN. Ivy, I'll say goodbye now.

IVY. You might show a *bit* of gratitude.

KEN. If you look at the Will. It's written on old paper in an old envelope. There was no message from God. Dad just didn't bother to change it.

IVY. God works in strange ways.

KEN. I think we've heard that before. Should you be driving?

IVY. I got here didn't I? I know when I'm not welcome.

KEN. The trouble is you don't.

IVY. Offensive to the bitter end.

(She heads for the exit.)

(Enter **RORY**, *ready to depart.)*

RORY. Ken!

KEN. What now?

RORY. Ken, are we goin'?

IVY. *(Defiant.)* Oh, there's something else! And you need to know! You'll be glad to know.

RORY. The manager's gimme the job.

KEN. You haven't even met him.

RORY. My mate showed him a selfie.

KEN. Just a selfie? Tell me it's not true. Wait outside. *(To* **IVY**.*)* I'm taking him to Blackpool, or maybe not. Thanks for bringing the clock.

IVY. *(To* **RORY**.*)* Oh, have we been formally introduced?

RORY. What's she sayin'?

KEN. Ivy, this is not a convenient time.

IVY. *(Urgent, whispering loudly to* **KEN**.*)* I've got something for you. It won't take long.

(From her bag she hands him a framed photo of his father, a captain in the army.)

Your father at his best, wearing his medals. Derek says it's rightfully yours.

(**KEN** *accepts the picture and places it next to the clock.*)

KEN. I still want the medals. I'll come to you.

IVY. He wasn't a bad man.

(**RORY** *looks at the photo.*)

RORY. Wow! Alpha dude! He'd be eaten alive in the gay village.

KEN. Get outside!

(*Text message ping on* **RORY**'s *phone. He goes out reading it.*)

IVY. There's more.

KEN. Photos?

IVY. I intended to write to you, but Derek says do it now. So, we said a prayer. We want to go to our graves with a clear conscience.

KEN. Well, it couldn't happen to a nicer couple. Go on.

RORY. (*Pops back in.*) Ken! He wants a take away. Chicken noodles, sweet and sour chicken, extra sauce.

(**KEN** *grabs* **RORY** *by the shoulders and frog marches him out of the room, whispering angrily in his ear. He comes back in and shuts the door.*)

KEN. His life is an action movie on fast forward. Attention span two seconds. Go on.

IVY. Kenneth, we're pleased you've got a friend.

KEN. The son of Satan?

IVY. You don't mean that. It's the physical thing, you see. Derek doesn't agree with it.

KEN. Derek's not gonna fuck him.

IVY. *(Stunned, as if she doesn't comprehend it.)* Oh, er... Kenneth, are you feeling alright? You were a late developer. We always worried about that. *(Beat.)* And we were very worried about the boxing. You loved boxing, but does boxing love you?

KEN. I know, my brain is a blancmange.

IVY. Are you still boxing? You'd better stop it then.

(**RORY** *pops his head round the door again.)*

RORY. The car's locked.

KEN. Wait in the hall. Two minutes.

RORY. I'm starving!

IVY. *(Calling after* **RORY**.) Young man, patience is a virtue!

KEN. You're wasting your breath. Say what you've got to say?

IVY. If you'll just hear me out. Y'know, when I were a girl, this room was my ballroom. My very own ballroom.

KEN. Yes, we know. The photo. You in your sugar-plum fairy dress. Go on. You've got five minutes.

IVY. Five minutes.

KEN. You can do it. God made the entire world in seven days.

IVY. Why take the Lord's name in vain so flippantly?

KEN. I don't believe in God. I believe in the Higgs boson particle. A scientific explanation for the creation of the Universe.

IVY. So, what's this Higgs thing?

KEN. Astrophysics. The Higgs boson particle binds molecules together to form solid matter. There you go. It's how the world was really formed.

IVY. I see. And who made the molecules?

KEN. *(Beat. He can't answer. Outburst.)* You said you had summat to tell me, Ivy! So tell me!

> (**KEN** *rushes to the window looking for* **RORY**.)

IVY. The boy's gone! He's just run out of the gate.

> (**KEN** *makes to run after him.*)

Let him go!

KEN. I promised him a lift. The weather.

IVY. You're smitten! Let him go his own way. He got this far by himself! Think what you're doing! What y'doin' standing there for? Please, sit down and listen. *(Beat.)* Let the lad go!

> *(Pause.)*

(Shouts.) You're too old for him!!

KEN. *(Sad.)* I like him.

> *(Pause.)*

IVY. *(Sympathetic.)* I know you do. I liked someone once. A long time ago. I grow old, but he stays young in my memory, and always will. It's life, Kenneth. There's always the one that got away. Your Dad's ashes are laid in the Glade of Remembrance.

KEN. Where's that?

IVY. Pray for him. You can't pray to a molecule.

KEN. You can pray to a bloody grapefruit, for all I care. What matters is where does it get you? What good's it done *you*?

IVY. It gives me the strength. The new medicine doesn't kill the pain. It only helps. Kenneth, don't question people's faith. It's sometimes all we have.

KEN. What did you want to tell me?

IVY. Don't be angry.

KEN. You mean don't go off on one. People keep telling me that.

IVY. You're too quick to find fault. Threatening Derek and me, abandoning your Father...

KEN. He threw me out, remember? The runt in a litter of one.

IVY. In the heat of the moment. Drunk. Learn to forgive.

KEN. "Are you courting, Kenneth? If not. Why not?" Over and over again, feeding his homophobia.

(*Pause. She is deep in regret.*)

So, who do I have to forgive? You? Dad? The Nazi bastard in the police showers?

IVY. May I continue? The Lord was merciful. Your Father died peacefully in his sleep.

KEN. As you do under sedation.

IVY. But something rather mysterious occurred. On the way into the hospice we were met by a doctor. She had a beautiful speaking voice like an oboe. She came forward and informed us that your Father was preparing to depart this life at any moment. They know these things. So, we waited through the night.

I thought he'd gone at one point. But suddenly he began to talk in a foreign language. That's what it sounded like, or gibberish. He'd never spoken anything but English? You know what he was like. He thought the Isle of Man was a foreign country. Anyway, it was no language I know of. He sat bolt upright and said, "What about my letter!" Well, Derek nearly fainted. How did he know we still had it? We couldn't send it to you. We didn't know where you were.

KEN. A letter?

IVY. *(With great difficulty.)* Kenneth, I apologize from the bottom of my heart! I had told Derek to burn it. Did your father know? Was he in touch with a higher power?

KEN. Suspicion. He knew what you're like. I won't go off on one. Just get out of the house!

> *(**KEN** gazes out of the window again.)*

> *(Pause.)*

IVY. Derek didn't burn it.

> *(She opens her bag and offers **KEN** the letter which has been torn open and re-sealed. He reads the letter.)*

Your father gives us leave to have something to remember him by. But keep the clock. We don't want to die in everlasting shame.

KEN. Remember him by? You went overboard.

IVY. We never planned to sell anything. We've plenty of room. Now, you're back home it's all worked out fine, hasn't it? Hasn't it, Kenneth?

> *(**KEN** is visibly upset by the letter.)*

Can we ever please you?

KEN. Did *he* write this?

> *(**IVY** waits by the door leaning on her stick.)*

IVY. Of course. Those last few minutes. The silence. A silence so deep, something had to happen. His hair was spread across the pillow, lit by sunbeams. His face, radiant and young again. Then we heard soft whispering sounds in that same strange language. Words floating in the air like prayers you could breathe in. Yes, it was the angels. Then he uttered his final words in this world. "Tell our Ken I didn't mean it."

(She exits.)

End of Scene Five

(A thunderstorm rages.)

Scene Six

(**RORY** *is seated wearing a bath towel round his shoulders. His bag is by his side. He rummages for a clean pair of jeans and another T-shirt. He's already put trackie bottoms on.*)

(**IVY** *enters carrying a bag of shopping.*)

IVY. Don't worry. This bag's been nowhere near the kitchen. I hear you're qualified in hygiene. Four cans of cola. One now, three for the road. Have you room in your knapsack?

(*She lays the four cans on the table.*)

You like cola, don't you?

RORY. Yeah. Thanks.

(*She looks at the window to see if* **KEN** *is coming home.*)

(**RORY** *opens a can of cola.*)

IVY. Put them in your knapsack. Or he'll shove them straight in that dirty fridge. You know what he's like.

RORY. Yeah, I do. Bad temper.

IVY. His own worst enemy when he's like this.

RORY. He's like it all the time.

IVY. When he sees you no arguments. Be nice to each other. Derek and me, we're always nice to each other. Some say we are each other's children.

RORY. Is he getting a take away or what?

IVY. He's looking for *you*. He won't go far. He'll think once you're on the motorway, you'll be gone. Ken wears his heart on his sleeve, other days he's a cold fish. I must go now. Derek's waiting.

(She heads for the door.)

RORY. Thanks for the coke.

IVY. You're in catering, aren't you?

RORY. Yeah, got a new job.

IVY. I often think this place could make a nice little guest house. I've always said so. Kenneth could do it up, if he had a mind to. If you've got any ideas. On catering, he certainly needs advice. A new kitchen for a start.

RORY. Enough microbes in there to start a new civilisation.

(A door slams off.)

*(**KEN** enters with more shopping.)*

KEN. *(Cheerful.)* I've been looking for you all over.

IVY. *(Pointing at **RORY**.)* Surprise, surprise!

KEN. Where did you find 'im?

IVY. Rather bedraggled under a tree. Scared stiff of lightning.

RORY. No I'm not.

KEN. *(Takes a pack of bottled of water out of the bag.)* I remembered what you said about the water. Tadpoles was it?

RORY. Sewage.

IVY. It's the rusty plumbing.

KEN. For you. I thought you'd scarpered but I still bought it. Coke. Funny how the mind works.

IVY. Funny how it doesn't.

KEN. I bet you <u>need</u> a drink...

RORY. *(Aloof.)* I've got one.

KEN. *(Suppressing his excitement.)* They keep bottled water in warehouses for months. Big business is buying up the water supply, the reservoirs and lakes. Fresh air next. If you live in the mountains, you'll have to pay fresh air tax.

RORY. Rant still not over. Change the bloody record.

IVY. No one can buy the rain clouds, can they? We've been talking about this being a guest house.

RORY. *You* were.

KEN. *(Snaps fingers.)* Nice one. He thinks it's the Psycho House.

IVY. Oh, stop all your doom and gloom!

KEN. All we've got is what's left of the world. Stick your head in the sand for much longer, your arse'll get sunburn.

IVY. I'll ignore that remark for the sake of goodwill. Good afternoon!

> *(**IVY** makes her exit.)*

KEN. I take it the job's not on?

RORY. I'm starvin'.

KEN. Let's go out somewhere. How about a cheeseburger, onion rings, chicken nuggets, double fries? You can overdose on vitamin Z. Anywhere but the motorway. There's a fish 'n' chip shop in the village. Quite a few good gastropubs. *(Beat.)* If you like, you can stay the night. No obligation, if you know what I mean.

> *(The front door slams shut.)*

> *(**RORY** sits on the sofa.)*

RORY. Did you really smack that twat in the shower?

KEN. *(Bravado.)* Oh yeah, yeah. *(He's lying.)* It sounded like a stick snapped. I thought I'd broken his neck. Knocked him down on the tiles. Two teeth fell out. A burst artery, blood everywhere. Then I jumped on him. They had to drag me off or he'd be dead.

(**KEN** *sits on the chaise longue.*)

RORY. You're a lousy liar. Too much detail.

(**KEN** *joins him on sofa.*)

(Silence, then...)

KEN. There's no obligation. WE can go any time you like.

RORY. *Another* knockback?

KEN. I mean it. No obligation if you want to stay a bit longer. Or is Blackpool off altogether. Plenty of clean bedding in the linen cupboard. Hot water's back on. I dunno what tea's like, made with sparkling water but I'll try anything once. Am I too old?

RORY. I like older. Straight acting in a pinstripe suit.

KEN. No Zombies then.

RORY. Zombies live in a swamp. They don't wear pinstripe.

KEN. A lot of business wives might disagree.

*(Silence. **RORY** is undecided.)*

Passive-aggressive. For fuck sake say something!

RORY. Ken, let's start a B&B.

KEN. I can't cook.

RORY. You know I can. I'll do the catering. You manage the business side. Do it up nice.

KEN. Primrose?

RORY. Defo. Start with the kitchen. You'll need a sand-blaster.

KEN. I'll get a *new* kitchen!

RORY. Then the bathrooms. Put showers in. Ensuite. We can charge more for boutique bedrooms. Artifical flowers in all the rooms. And you've got a gay B&B. Birdin', cyclin', walkin'.

KEN. Artificial flowers?

RORY. I like the way they don't grow,

KEN. A gay B&B? You can't turn straights away. It's against the law. Anyway, what's the difference between a gay B&B and any other?

RORY. Candlelight breakfast.

KEN. Would you by any chance be talking your way into a job?

RORY. And get a dog. Security. Can we fetch Brindle now?

KEN. *(Tentative.)* You want me to drive to London and fetch Brindle here? What will your dad say?

RORY. S'up to you.

KEN. I'd better charge up the car. A gay B&B. Good location. But no tours of moors murders graves.

(**RORY** *starts getting dressed excitedly.*)

RORY. Murder is good for business. Just sayin'. If you don't like the idea...

KEN. I'm only in a sweat, hot flushes palpitations. My heart is bouncing around like a tennis ball. Is this your idea or...?

RORY. The witch.

KEN. I didn't tell you, but after the incident in the shower, I went for counselling. On orders of the Super. Private psychologist, older than I expected, but good-hearted. She told me to stop bashing people and have more sex instead. That's not so easy. I haven't got a boyfriend.

No compunction, she said: "The male population of the world is four billion. See you next week."

RORY. When was that?

KEN. Yesterday.

> (**KEN** *darts out of the room unseen by* **RORY**, *who's drying his hair.*)

RORY. I'm under a tree, thunder and nine colours of fuckin' lightnin', right? The witch turns up in her car. Hop in. So, I'm thinkin' what she up to? Dropping me on the motorway? No answer, she does a nifty u-turn and comes straight back here.

The interview, I reckon it's a set up. Set up for that manager's personal delicament. Yeah, set up! Me mate pimping me! *(Beat.)* He can stuff his fuckin' Red Bombers and make do with paracetamol. Serves 'im right. You won't believe me. What I actually done is chuck 'em in a river. Watch out for flying fish. *(Beat.)* So, Ken, can I sleep in your bed with you?

> (**KEN** *reappears naked from the waist up, wearing a police officer's cap. He leans casually on the doorpost.*)

KEN. Ahem...

RORY. She-yit! Detective Sergeant...

KEN. Anything but fuckin' Spiderman.

RORY. That police cap! Is it real?

KEN. Defo. It ain't fancy dress. They won't miss it.

RORY. Are we rockin'?

KEN. No drugs, Roy.

RORY. Rory *(Beat.)* Are y'gonna fuck me?

The End

ABOUT THE AUTHOR

James Hogan wrote a number of plays between the late '70s to the early '90s, performed at various fringe venues such as the Gate Theatre, the Cockpit, the Old Red Lion, the Kings Head in London and the Edinburgh Festival. Out of his work as a reader for the Royal Court and an organiser of the writers group at the Riverside Studios, he founded Oberon Books in 1986. Oberon championed plays by unknown writers, publishing them in high quality editions, a total of over 200 works. Oberon Books was sold to Bloomsbury publishing in 2019. James's play *Ivy & Joan* is also published by Samuel French.